LOOPDELOOM™

SPINNING LOOM MAKES WEAVING FAST AND FUN

Once you see how fast and fun it is to weave the accessories in this creative collection, you'll be wild about the Loopdeloom™! Using yarn, ribbon, or other fibers, the possibilities are endless! For information about choosing yarn, making pom-poms and tassels, and great hints and tips, turn to pages 26-28.

TABLE OF CONTENTS

LEISURE ARTS, INC. • Maumelle, AR

HEADBAND

SHOPPING LIST

- ☐ 8 yards Super Bulky (6) weight yarn (We used a pink/ orange/purple variegated yarn.)
- ☐ 20 yards Medium (4) weight yarn (We used an orange yarn.)
- ☐ 7 yards Super Bulky (6) weight yarn (We used a pink bumpy yarn.)
- ☐ 6" length of 1" wide foldover elastic
- ☐ plastic yarn needle

Woven on just 5 pegs, this bold-colored headband can also serve as an ear warmer. Adding elastic at the back of the 17" long headband makes it one-size-fits-all. What a great gift idea!

to make the headband

Refer to the Basic Instructions booklet that came with the Loopdeloom™ while making your headband. Read the General Instructions in this book, starting on page 26.

1. Cut 5 54" orange yarn lengths for the warp strands. Insert 5 pegs on the loom and place the warp strands on the pegs.
2. Weave the variegated yarn for 2". Change to the orange yarn.
3. Weave the orange yarn for 1". Change to the pink bumpy yarn.
4. Weave the pink bumpy yarn for 1". Change to the orange yarn.
5. Weave the orange yarn for 1". Change to the variegated yarn.
6. Repeat Steps 2-5 twice more. Weave the variegated yarn for 2".
7. After completing the woven portion and removing it from the pegs, knot all the warp strands together at each end. Knot the foldover elastic to each end and adjust to fit. Trim the yarn and elastic ends to about 3/4".

PHONE CASE

SHOPPING LIST

- ☐ 45 yards Bulky (5) weight yarn (We used pink/grey/black variegated yarn.)
- ☐ plastic yarn needle
- ☐ scrap of cardboard

THIS VARIEGATED YARN MAKES IT LOOK LIKE YOU USED 3 DIFFERENT YARNS, BUT THE WEAVING IS QUICK WITH ONE CONTINUOUS STRAND WOVEN ON 7 PEGS!

THE PHONE CASE MEASURES ABOUT 3" WIDE AND 5" LONG.

to make the phone case

REFER TO THE BASIC INSTRUCTIONS BOOKLET THAT CAME WITH THE LOOPDELOOM™ WHILE MAKING YOUR PHONE CASE. READ THE GENERAL INSTRUCTIONS IN THIS BOOK, STARTING ON PAGE 26.

1. Cut 7 44" yarn lengths for the warp strands. Insert 7 pegs on the loom and place the warp strands on the pegs.
2. Weave the yarn for 12".
3. After completing the woven portion and removing it from the pegs, knot the warp strands and trim to about 1". Match the short ends and fold the piece in half. Use the yarn needle and yarn to whipstitch the side seams, leaving the top 1" open at each side.
4. For the cuff, fold over the top edges and whipstitch in place, tucking the warp strands under the cuff as you sew.
5. Make 2 pom-poms and sew them to a side seam.

TFW 3G
100%
3:23
Thursday, August 28

SCARF

SHOPPING LIST

- ☐ 80 yards Bulky (5) weight yarn (We used a grey yarn.)
- ☐ 80 yards Bulky (5) weight yarn (We used a magenta/gold/purple variegated yarn.)
- ☐ 108 yards Medium (4) weight yarn (We used a purple tone-on-tone yarn.)
- ☐ plastic yarn needle

Woven on all 15 pegs, this striped scarf can be made in lots of color and yarn combinations.

The scarf measures about 6½" wide and 45" long.

to make the scarf

Refer to the Basic Instructions booklet that came with the LoopdeLoom™ while making your scarf.Read the General Instructions in this book, starting on page 26.

1. Cut 5 110" lengths of **each** yarn for the warp strands. Insert 15 pegs on the loom and place the warp strands on the pegs, alternating the grey, variegated, and purple strands.
2. Weave the grey yarn for 3". Change to the purple yarn.
3. Weave the purple yarn for 1". Change to the variegated yarn.
4. Weave the variegated yarn for 2". Change to the purple yarn.
5. Weave the purple yarn for 1". Change to the grey yarn.
6. Repeat Steps 2-5 five times more. Weave the grey yarn for 3".
7. After completing the woven portion and removing it from the pegs, knot the warp strands and trim to about 3".

Bracelets

Shopping List

For each Bracelet:

- ☐ 3 yards Medium (4) or Bulky (5) weight yarn for the warp strands (We used a pink yarn, an orange yarn, and a purple yarn.)
- ☐ 3-5 yards Super Bulky (5) weight yarn or 3/8" wide satin ribbon (We used a pink sequined ribbon-style yarn, a pink/purple/gold variegated yarn, and a magenta satin ribbon.)

Pick 2 yarns (or a yarn and a ribbon) and weave them on 3 pegs for fun, fashionable cuff-style bracelets! See the descriptions under the photo on page 9.

to make each bracelet

Refer to the Basic Instructions booklet that came with the LoopDeLoom™ while making your bracelets. Read the General Instructions in this book, starting on page 26.

1. For a 7" long bracelet, cut 3 34" yarn lengths for the warp strands. Insert 3 pegs on the loom and place the warp strands on the pegs.
2. Weave the yarn for 7". If you are using 2 yarns (or a yarn and a ribbon) for weaving, hold the 2 strands together as 1 while you weave.
3. After completing the woven portion and removing it from the pegs, knot all the warp strands together at each end, leaving the strands long enough to tie the bracelet on your wrist.

Upper Left: The pink sequined ribbon-style yarn bracelet has a bulky weight pink yarn for the warp strands. Lower Left: Purple medium weight yarn is used for the warp strands and is held together with the variegated yarn while weaving the bracelet.

Upper Right: Weave satin ribbon and meduim weight purple yarn on purple yarn warp strands for the twisted-center bracelet (just twist the center before tying the bracelet on your wrist). Lower Right: The bracelet starts with orange medium weight yarn warp strands and is woven with the orange yarn held alongside a pink sequined ribbon-style yarn.

MUG RUG & COASTER

SHOPPING LIST

For the Mug Rug:

- ☐ 20 yards Super Bulky (6) yarn (We used a brown variegated yarn.)
- ☐ 32 yards Medium (4) weight yarn (We used an orange yarn.)
- ☐ plastic yarn needle

For each Coaster:

- ☐ 7 yards Super Bulky (6) yarn (We used a brown variegated yarn.)
- ☐ 14 yards Medium (4) weight yarn (We used an orange yarn.)
- ☐ plastic yarn needle

PICK 2 YARNS AND WEAVE A MUG RUG AND MATCHING COASTERS.
THE MUG RUG IS FRINGED WHILE THE COASTER ENDS ARE NEATLY WOVEN IN.

MUG RUG APPROXIMATE SIZE: 8$^1/_2$" WIDE AND 6$^1/_2$" HIGH
COASTER APPROXIMATE SIZE: 4" SQUARE

REFER TO THE BASIC INSTRUCTIONS BOOKLET THAT CAME WITH THE LOOPDELOOM™ WHILE MAKING YOUR MUG RUG AND COASTER. READ THE GENERAL INSTRUCTIONS IN THIS BOOK, STARTING ON PAGE 26.

to make the mug rug

1. Cut 15 37" orange yarn lengths for the warp strands. Insert 15 pegs on a loom and place the warp strands on the pegs.
2. Weave the orange yarn for 1". Change to the brown yarn.
3. Weave the brown yarn for 6$^1/_2$". Change to the orange yarn.
4. Weave the orange yarn for 1".
5. After completing the woven portion and removing it from the pegs, knot the warp strands and trim to about 1$^1/_2$".

to make each coaster

1. Cut 9 28" orange yarn lengths for the warp strands. Insert 9 pegs on a loom and place the warp strands on the pegs.
2. Weave the orange yarn for 1/2". Change to the brown yarn.
3. Weave the brown yarn for 3". Change to the orange yarn.
4. Weave the orange yarn for 1/2".
5. After completing the woven portion and removing it from the pegs, weave the warp strands into the coaster.

WASHCLOTH

SHOPPING LIST

For each Washcloth:

- ☐ 50 yards Medium (MEDIUM 4) weight cotton yarn for the main color (We used a grey yarn and a blue yarn.)
- ☐ 7 yards Medium (MEDIUM 4) weight cotton yarn for the stripe (We used a blue yarn and a grey yarn.)
- ☐ plastic yarn needle

COTTON YARN WEAVES UP INTO BUTTERY-SOFT WASHCLOTHS. A SIMPLE STRIPE ACCENTS THE 6$^1/_2$" SQUARE CLOTH.

to make the washcloth

REFER TO THE BASIC INSTRUCTIONS BOOKLET THAT CAME WITH THE LOOPDELOOM™ WHILE MAKING YOUR WASHCLOTH. READ THE GENERAL INSTRUCTIONS IN THIS BOOK, STARTING ON PAGE 26.

1. Cut 15 33" main color yarn lengths for the warp strands. Insert 15 pegs on a loom and place the warp strands on the pegs.
2. Weave the main color yarn for 2$^3/_4$". Change to the stripe color yarn.
3. Weave the stripe color yarn for 1". Change to the main color yarn.
4. Weave the main color yarn for 2$^3/_4$" more.
5. After completing the woven portion and removing it from the pegs, knot the warp strands and trim to about 1$^1/_4$".

COWL

SHOPPING LIST

- ☐ 315 yards Medium (4) weight yarn (We used a blue/purple/magenta/grey variegated yarn.)
- ☐ $2^1/_4$" dia. button
- ☐ 22mm sew-on snap
- ☐ sewing needle and thread
- ☐ plastic yarn needle

THIS PROJECT IS CREATED WITH 2 LOOPDELOOM™ LOOMS.

THE SUBTLE COLOR CHANGES IN THIS VARIEGATED YARN MAKE SUCH A PRETTY COWL, AND THE ADDITION OF THE OVERSIZE BUTTON TAKES IT TO THE NEXT LEVEL. FOR A DIFFERENT LOOK, MAKE THE COWL IN A BRIGHT SOLID COLOR AND USE A CONTRASTING COLOR BUTTON FOR AN EYE-CATCHING TOUCH!

THE COWL IS WOVEN ON 23 PEGS AND IS ABOUT $10^1/_2$" WIDE AND 33" LONG.

to make the cowl

REFER TO THE BASIC INSTRUCTIONS BOOKLET THAT CAME WITH THE LOOPDELOOM™ WHILE MAKING YOUR COWL. READ THE GENERAL INSTRUCTIONS IN THIS BOOK, STARTING ON PAGE 26.

1. Join 2 looms. Cut 23 86" yarn lengths for the warp strands. Insert 23 pegs on the looms and place the warp strands on the pegs. Weave the yarn for 33".
2. After completing the woven portion and removing it from the pegs, knot the warp strands and trim to about $2^1/_2$".
3. Wrap the cowl around your neck and place a pin where you want the button to be. Use the yarn and yarn needle to sew the button to the cowl. Use the sewing needle and thread to sew the snap to the cowl under the button.

PURSE

SHOPPING LIST

- ☐ 240 yards Bulky (BULKY 5) weight yarn (We used a brown yarn for purse and strap.)
- ☐ 20 yards Bulky (BULKY 5) weight yarn (We used a blue yarn.)
- ☐ 30 yards Bulky (BULKY 5) weight yarn (We used an orange yarn.)
- ☐ 25 yards Bulky (BULKY 5) weight yarn (We used a lime green bumpy yarn.)
- ☐ 35 yards Bulky (BULKY 5) weight yarn (We used a an orange/yellow variegated bumpy yarn.)
- ☐ 35 yards Bulky (BULKY 5) weight yarn (We used a blue/brown/gold/green variegated yarn.)
- ☐ plastic yarn needle

THIS PROJECT IS CREATED WITH 2 LOOPDELOOM™ LOOMS.

JOIN 2 LOOMS AND WEAVE STRIPES INTO THIS BOHO PURSE. SUBSTITUTE SOFT PINKS AND VIOLETS FOR A ROMANTIC LOOK OR NEUTRAL TONES FOR A NATURAL STYLE!

THE PURSE IS ABOUT 10" WIDE AND 11" LONG, NOT INCLUDING THE STRAP.

to make the purse

REFER TO THE BASIC INSTRUCTIONS BOOKLET THAT CAME WITH THE LOOPDELOOM™ WHILE MAKING YOUR PURSE. READ THE GENERAL INSTRUCTIONS IN THIS BOOK, STARTING ON PAGE 26.

1. For the purse body, join 2 looms. Cut 30 60" brown yarn lengths for the warp strands. Insert 30 pegs on the looms and place the warp strands on the pegs.
2. Weave the brown yarn for about 1 1/2". Change to another yarn.
3. Weave the other yarn for 1/2"-1 1/2". Change to another yarn.
4. Repeat Step 3 until the woven portion is about 19" long. Change to brown and weave the brown yarn for about 1 1/2".

5. After completing the woven portion and removing it from the pegs, fold the piece in half, matching the right sides and short ends. Make a knotted seam. Use the yarn needle and yarn to whipstitch the bottom seam. Turn the purse right side out and fold over the top edge about 2" for a cuff.

6. For the purse strap, cut 5 88" brown yarn lengths for the warp strands. Insert 5 pegs on a loom and place the warp strands on the pegs.

7. Weave the brown yarn for about 34".

8. After completing the woven portion and removing it from the pegs, knot the warp strands. Use the yarn needle and yarn to sew the strap inside the purse top.

PILLOW

SHOPPING LIST

- ☐ 190 yards Super Bulky (SUPER BULKY 6) weight yarn (We used a mauve/burgundy/brown/green variegated chenille yarn.)
- ☐ 50 yards Bulky (BULKY 5) weight yarn (We used a lime green bumpy yarn.)
- ☐ 12" square pillow form
- ☐ plastic yarn needle

THIS PROJECT IS CREATED WITH 2 LOOPDELOOM™ LOOMS.

JOIN 2 LOOMS TOGETHER TO WEAVE A 14" SQUARE. WE USED THE SAME YARNS AND STRIPING SEQUENCE ON BOTH THE FRONT AND BACK OF THE PILLOW. MIX IT UP BY CHANGING THE STRIPING SEQUENCE ON ONE SIDE OR BY WEAVING 2 TOTALLY DIFFERENT YARNS FOR A 2-FOR-1 PILLOW!

to make the pillow

REFER TO THE BASIC INSTRUCTIONS BOOKLET THAT CAME WITH THE LOOPDELOOM™ WHILE MAKING YOUR PILLOW. READ THE GENERAL INSTRUCTIONS IN THIS BOOK, STARTING ON PAGE 26.

1. For the Pillow front, join 2 looms. Cut 30 48" lengths of the variegated yarn for the warp strands. Insert 30 pegs on the looms and place the warp strands on the pegs.
2. Weave the variegated yarn for 4 1/2". Change to the green yarn.
3. Weave the green yarn for 1 1/2". Change to the variegated yarn.
4. Weave the variegated yarn for 2". Change to the green yarn.
5. Weave the green yarn for 1 1/2". Change to the variegated yarn.
6. Weave the variegated yarn for 4 1/2". Remove the woven portion from the pegs.
7. Repeat Steps 1-6 to make the Pillow back.
8. After completing the front and back, place the pieces right sides together and use the yarn needle and variegated yarn to sew the finished edges together. Turn the Pillow right side out and make knotted seams on the sides, inserting the pillow form before you knot the last side.

Place Mat

Shopping List

- ☐ 94 yards Super Bulky (6) weight yarn (We used a black and white twist yarn.)
- ☐ 65 yards Medium (4) weight yarn (We used a black yarn.)
- ☐ 65 yards Bulky (5) weight yarn (We used a white bumpy yarn.)
- ☐ plastic yarn needle

This project is created with 2 Loopdeloom™ looms.

Woven on 2 looms, this striped place mat looks very modern in black and white. A set of place mats woven in holiday colors makes a great gift.

Approximate Size: 18½" wide (excluding the fringe) and 13" high

to make the place mat

Refer to the Basic Instructions booklet that came with the Loopdeloom™ while making your place mat. Read the General Instructions in this book, starting on page 26.

1. Join 2 looms. Cut 30 58" black/white yarn lengths for the warp strands. Insert 30 pegs on the looms and place the warp strands on the pegs.
2. Weave the black/white yarn for 2". Change to the black yarn.
3. Weave the black yarn for ¾". Change to the white yarn.
4. Weave the white yarn for 2". Change to the black yarn.
5. Weave the black yarn for ¾". Change to the black/white yarn.
6. Repeat Steps 2-5 twice more. Weave 2" of the black/white yarn.
7. After completing the woven portion and removing it from the pegs, knot the warp strands and trim to about 2".

Plastic Bag Purse

Shopping List

- ☐ 3-4 33-gallon trash bags (We used clear bags.)
- ☐ 1 39-gallon trash bag (We used a black bag.)
- ☐ plastic yarn needle
- ☐ scrap of cardboard

This project is created with 2 LoopdeLoom™ looms.

Trash bags never looked so good! Cut continuous strips from the plastic bags and weave a bright purse.

to make the purse

Refer to the Basic Instructions booklet that came with the LoopdeLoom™ while making your purse. Read the General Instructions in this book, starting on page 26.

1. To cut **each** trash bag into continuous strips, cut off the bottom seam and any handles or drawstrings. Unfold the bag and lay the tube flat on your work surface with the open ends at the sides. Beginning at one open end, mark the folded edges in $1^{1}/_{2}$" increments with a pen. Repeat on the other folded edge of the tube. Open the tube. Cut diagonally toward the first mark on the opposite side, cutting only through one layer of the bag; continue cutting the tube into a long continuous strip, using the marks as a guide *(Fig. 1)*. Cut off the pointed ends. Cut about 200 yards of clear strips and 30 yards of black strips.

Fig. 1

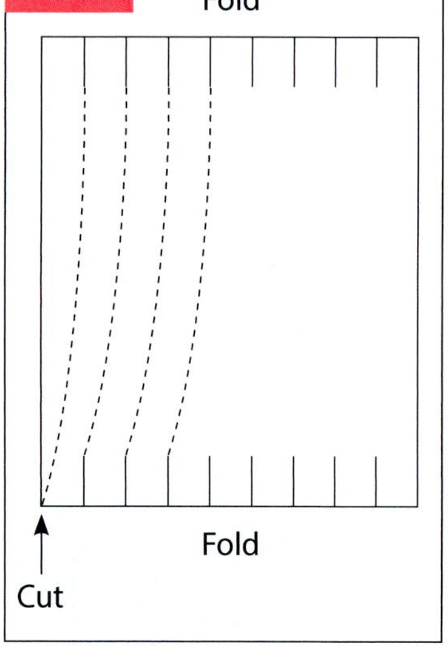

2 As you weave, you will need to add new strips to continue weaving or to change colors. To join a new strip, cut a 1/2" slit, about 3/4" from the ends of both strips *(Fig. 2)*. Place the end of one strip over the end of another strip and match the slits. Pull the free end of the top strip through both slits from the bottom to the top *(Fig. 3)*. Pull the strips gently to form a small knot.

FIG. 2

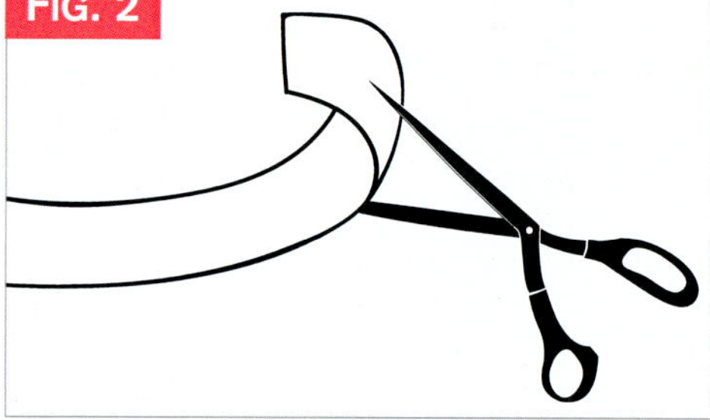

FIG. 3

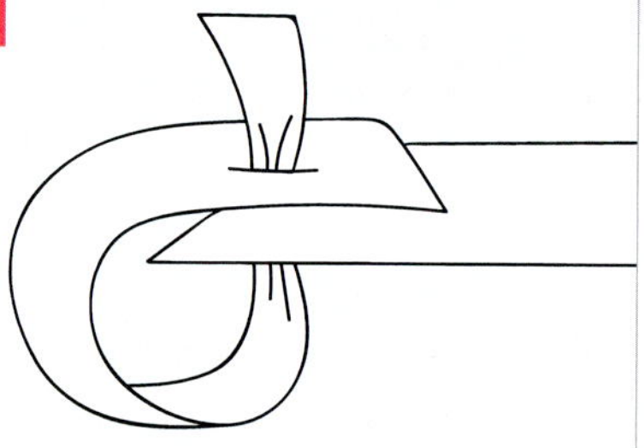

3 For the purse body, join 2 looms and insert 30 pegs. Cut 30 71" clear bag strips for the warp strands. Place the warp strands on the pegs.

4 Weave the clear strips for about 5". Change to the black strips.

5 Weave the black strips for 2 1/4". Change to clear strips.

6 Weave the clear strips for 11". Change to the black strips.

7 Weave the black strips for 2 1/4". Change to the clear strips.

8 Weave the clear strips for 5". After completing the woven portion and removing it from the pegs, knot the warp strands and trim to about 1". Match the short ends of the piece and fold in half. Use the yarn needle and matching color strips to whipstitch the side edges together.

9 To shape the bag bottom, flatten and center one side seam against the bottom of the purse; use the yarn needle and a clear strip to sew across the corner $1^1/_2$" from the point *(Fig. 4)*. Repeat for the remaining corner. Turn the purse right side out.

FIG. 4

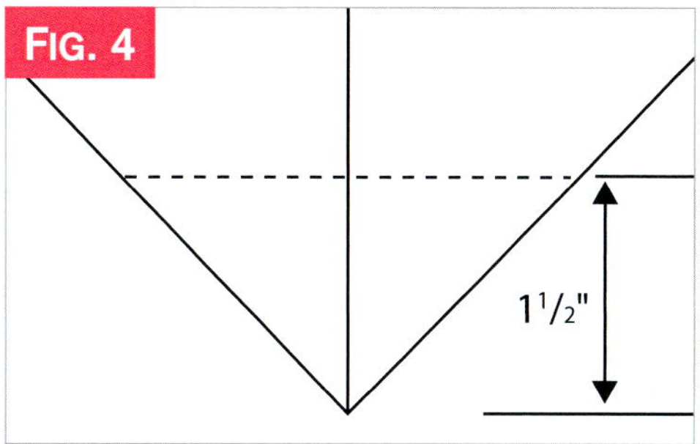

10 For each purse handle, cut six 18" clear strips. Holding all strips together, tie an overhand knot close to one end. Divide the strips into 3 groups of 2 strips each and braid the strips. Knot near the ends. Insert the strap knots into the purse, about 3" from the top and 4" from each side *(Fig. 5)*. Securely sew in place with the yarn needle and a clear strip.

FIG. 5

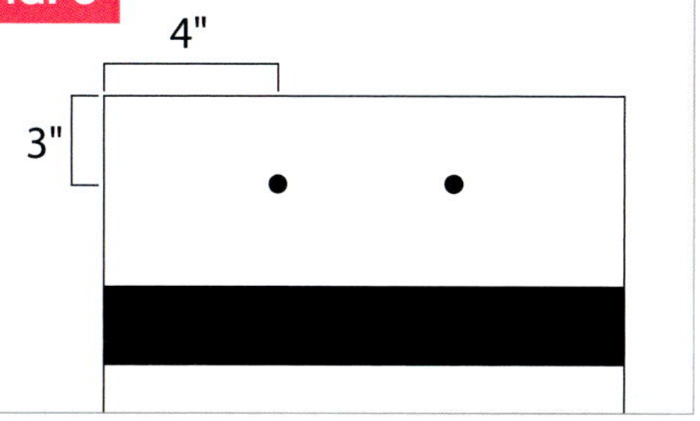

11 Fold the top edge of the purse 2" to the inside and whipstitch in place with the yarn needle and clear strips, covering the knots on the handles and tucking the warp strands under the hem as you sew.

12 Make a tassel with clear and black strips; tie the tassel to one handle.

General Instructions

Selecting Your Yarn

A listing of the specific yarns used for the projects in this book can be found at www.leisurearts.com/6495.pdf

Your first step is to choose yarn. Yarn is sold in skeins and may be thick, thin, or somewhere in between. Most skeins of yarn will have a little yarn skein symbol with a number on it. The higher the number, the thicker the yarn. Here's a reference guide for yarn sizes:

- Super Fine; also called Sock, Fingering, Baby
- Fine; also called Sport, Baby
- Light; also called DK, Light Medium
- Medium; also called Worsted, Afghan, Aran
- Bulky; also called Chunky, Craft, Rug
- Super Bulky; also called Bulky, Roving

Any yarn can be used for the weft, but some Bulky or Super Bulky yarns may not work as warp strands because they may not fit in the peg guides. In these situations, just use a thinner yarn for the warp strands.

It's fun to mix colors, sizes, and textures of yarn. Check the project instructions for the type of yarn and amount we used.

When mixing yarns, be sure to check the washing and care instructions. If your project will be washed, be sure to choose washable yarns. We recommend hand washing your project and allowing it to dry flat.

Don't feel limited to just yarn. Experiment with ribbon, embroidery floss, or even strips cut from plastic bags!

Yarn pom-poms and tassels are a fun way to embellish your project. See the instructions on page 27.

Weaving in Warp Strands

Thread the warp strands at one end on a plastic yarn needle. Going **over** the first woven loop, weave the warp ends into the woven portion; come out of the woven portion *(Figs. 1-2)*.

Fig. 1

Fig. 2

Skipping every other set of warp strands, use the yarn needle to weave the warp strands *(Fig. 3)*. Trim the woven ends.

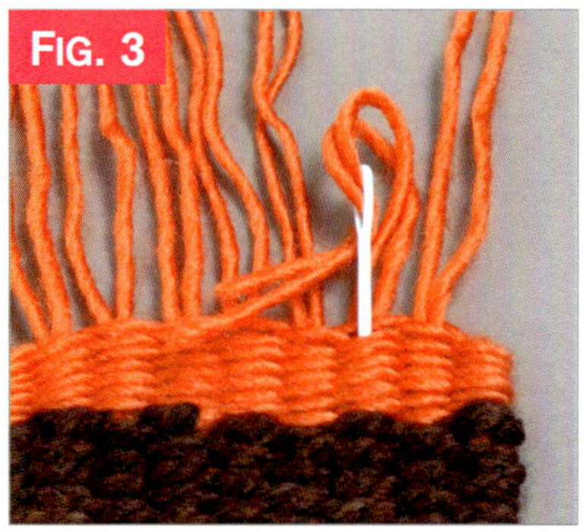
Fig. 3

Turn the project to the other side and use the yarn needle to weave in the remaining warp ends *(Fig. 4)*.

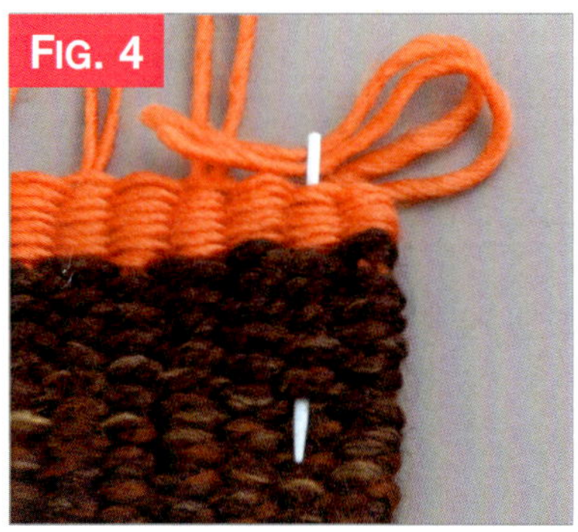
Fig. 4

Pom-Pom

Cut a piece of cardboard 3" x 5". Wrap the yarn around the cardboard about 34 times *(Fig. 5)*.

FIG. 5

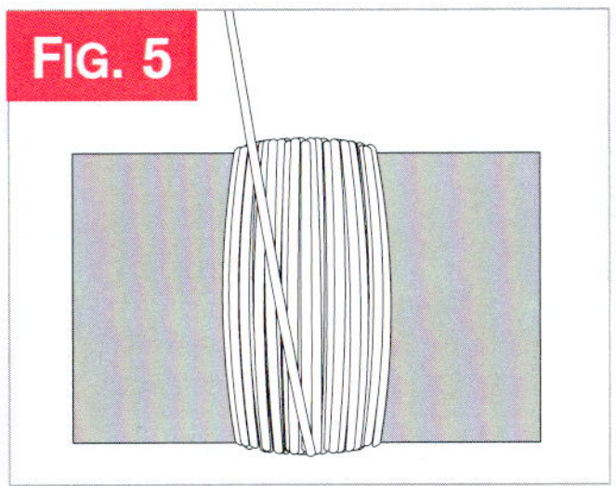

Carefully slip the yarn off the cardboard and firmly tie an 18" yarn length around the middle *(Fig. 6)*.

FIG. 6

Leave the yarn ends long enough to attach the pom-pom. Cut the loops on both ends and trim the pom-pom into a smooth ball *(Fig. 7)*. Thread a yarn needle with the long ends and sew the pom-pom to your project.

FIG. 7

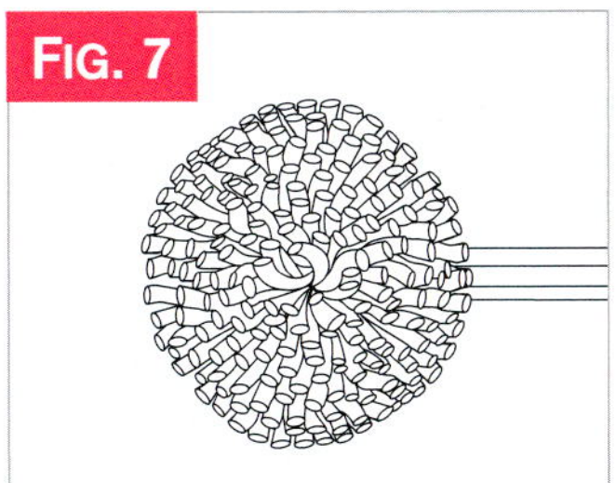

Tassel

Cut a piece of cardboard 3" x 4". Wrap a clear bag strip around the cardboard 8 times. Wrap a black bag strip around the cardboard 4 times. Cut an 8" black bag strip and insert it under all of the strands at the top of the cardboard; pull up. Cut the strips at the opposite end of the cardboard and then remove the tassel *(Fig. 8)*.

FIG. 8

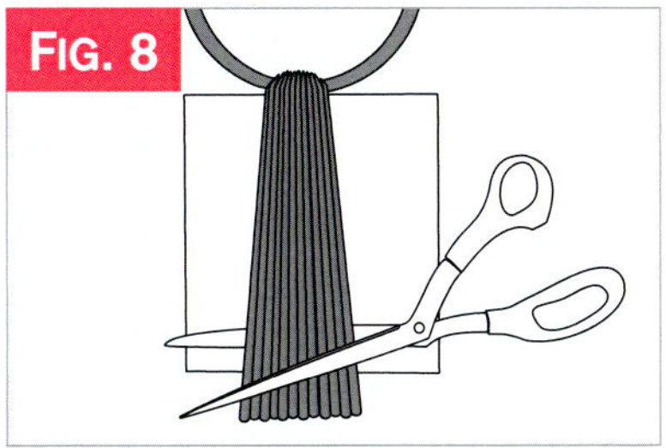

Cut a 12" black strip length and wrap it tightly around the tassel twice, $^{1}/_{2}$" below the top *(Fig. 9)*; tie securely and trim the ends. Trim the tassel ends as desired.

FIG. 9

HINTS & TIPS

- On our projects, we cut the warp strands twice as long as the finished project plus 20". The extra yarn at the ends ensures that you don't pull the warp strands out when you are advancing the woven portion.
- Do not cut the weft strands; work from the yarn skein when weaving.
- Leave a 6" weft tail when you start and finish weaving. Knot this tail in with the warp threads.
- When replacing the peg into the base after advancing the woven portion, be sure that the warp yarn doesn't get looped or caught on an adjacent peg *(Figs. 10-11)*.

Incorrect: *Warp strand looped over an adjacent peg.*

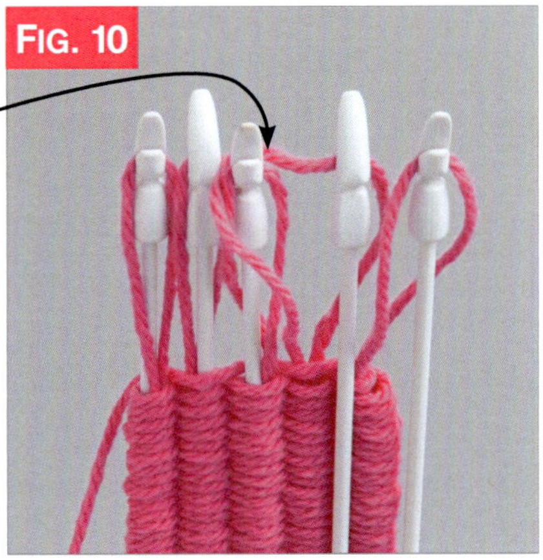

FIG. 10

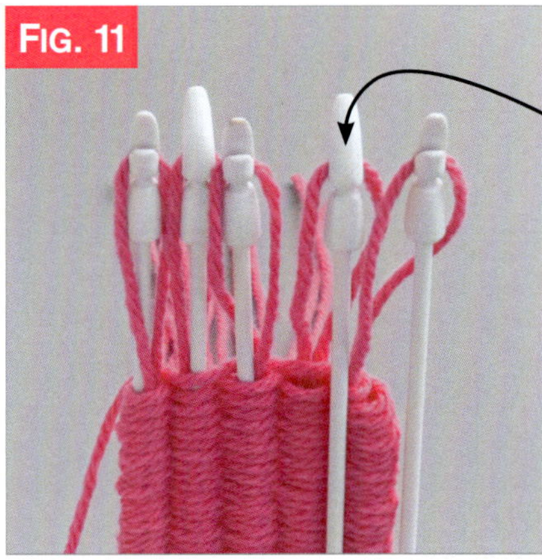

FIG. 11

Correct: *Warp strand looped on a single peg.*

- Change colors or add a new yarn by securely knotting the yarn ends together. Once your project is complete and off the loom, hide the yarn ends by using a yarn needle to weave the ends into the woven portion.
- Push the yarn down and tighten the woven area as you work.
- As you weave, periodically arrange and pull the warp threads taut behind the loom(s).
- Smooth and adjust the woven areas of the project after you knot or weave in the warp ends.

Production Team: Designer – Kelly Reider; Technical Writer – Mary Sullivan Hutcheson; Technical Associates – Lisa Lancaster and Jean Lewis; Editorial Writer – Susan Frantz Wiles; Senior Graphic Artist – Lora Puls; Graphic Artist – Cailen Cochran; Photostylist – Lori Wenger; Photographers – Jason Masters and Ken West.